FEATURING THE ARTWORK OF

THOMAS
KINKADE

BESIDE STILL WATERS

Published in Nashville, TN

by Thomas Nelson, Inc.

Text in this work were selected from

Soul Searching.

Originally published as a four-volume set, *Seasons of Life Meditations*.

Published by Thomas Nelson, Inc. © 1994

ISBN 0-7852-6844-8

Design and production by: Quebecor World Digital Services, Chicago

Printed in the United States of America

1 2 3 4 5 6 - 05 04 03 02 01 00

FEATURING THE ARTWORK OF

THOMAS
KINKADE

BESIDE STILL WATERS

THOMAS NELSON PUBLISHERS®
Nashville

When April with its
gentle showers has pierced
the March drought to the
root and bathed every plant
in the moisture . . . when . . .
small birds sing melodiously,
so touched in their hearts
by nature that they sleep
all night with open
eyes—then folks long to
go on pilgrimages.

—Geoffrey Chaucer

Winter's over. (Well, almost.) Sun's out (when it's not pouring rain). Air is warmer. Grass is turning green. Birds are getting busy. And I feel the urge to get busy too—to build something, grow something, clean something, make something, or just to get outside and move.

This stirring, no doubt, is biological, the result of being cooped up for too long. It's partially a primitive physiological response to longer days and more sunlight. But I think it's also a divine nudge— an impulse from my Creator to be about the business I was put on earth for.

And there's the rub, because I'm not always certain what that business is! Spring has given me the gift of renewed energy and a spurt of new hope, but I'm not clear what to do next. Maybe that's why my gardens often get planned but not plowed, my exercise programs don't last, my spring cleaning gets interrupted and goes unfinished.

Maybe before I fling open the door and run outside, I need to spend some time inside . . . inside me. Before I get busy with whatever projects offer themselves, maybe I need to go on an inner pilgrimage, to spend some time in journaling and prayer, to meditate on purpose and direction. I need to pray . . .

Prayer: My God, You gave me this restlessness, this urge to get busy. Grant me the purpose to know what I need to do with it and the courage and commitment to follow through even when this surge of energy ebbs.

Thomas Kinkade

Love lives again, that
with the dead has been:
Love is come again like
wheat that springeth green.

—John Macleod Campbell Crum

There's something about pain that just freezes a person up. When we've been hurt, when we've lost something or somebody we loved, we tend to tighten up, to shut down emotionally.

And this is not necessarily bad. Human protective mechanisms exist for a purpose. Psychologists tell us that depression is a normal and necessary response to loss; it's the body's way of slowing life down so that thoughts and feelings have time to adjust.

Just as winter allows the earth time to rest and prepare for new growth, emotional withdrawal can buy time for a wounded self to heal. But we can't stay frozen forever. We have to let ourselves thaw out.

A spring thaw can be gradual and gentle, the slow unfolding of a blossoming soul. Or it can be sudden and violent, like ice floes snapping and spring thunderstorms roaring. But with the thaw, sudden or gentle, comes release and the promise of greener days ahead.

It is with this emotional thaw, that we realize the grace of God and His loving mercy have been sustaining us through the difficult times.

Prayer: Lord, I need emotional defenses. But eventually I also need the grace and courage to let them go.

Now to Him who is able
to do exceedingly abundantly
above all that we ask or
think . . . to Him be glory.

—*Ephesians 3:20–21*

Magazine articles and pop psychology books are always cautioning me about my expectations. Apparently many of my problems (and everybody else's problems) result from unrealistic, unexamined expectations.

Do I expect approval for what I do and what I am? I'd better find another source of self-esteem.

Do I expect people to read my mind? I'd better learn to communicate my wants and needs.

Do I expect life to be fair or even happy? I'd better get real!

And all this is helpful to a point. But after awhile I start wondering exactly what I *can* expect. Something deep within me rebels at the cynicism of the apparent message: "Expect nothing; that way you won't be disappointed."

So what *can* I reasonably expect from my life and my relationships? As far as I can tell, these are the basics:

- In this world, I can expect to have problems—sickness, rejection, tragedy, interrupted plans.

- I can expect God to be with me through it all. I can count on God's comfort and God's strength if I can remember to keep turning to Him.
- I can expect that eventually, over the long term, things will work out for the best. Not necessarily the way I planned. Not necessarily in ways I can see at the time. Not necessarily even in my lifetime. But I can reasonably expect that God will remain in charge and will continue to be good and loving.
- I can expect to be surprised with even more than I ever thought to expect—more than I could ask for or think about—if I keep myself focused on God's purposes.

Prayer: Exactly how this all works is a mystery— I can't expect to understand it all. But I can trust You, Lord, to be with me as I learn to adjust my expectations.

*Those who sow in
tears shall reap in joy.*

—*Psalm 126:5*

A man on our street when I was growing up took all the grass out of his front yard and replaced it with gravel. He had a heart condition and wasn't supposed to do yard work. I can understand that. Besides, rock gardens look great.

But the strange thing was that this man insisted on green gravel. And he was the crankiest neighbor of all about keeping kids off his "lawn." Although he skipped the work of sodding and fertilizing and mowing, it seemed he still wanted to convince himself and others that he was growing grass. Of course, he wasn't fooling anybody. And he still had to do the work of defending his turf.

I think I sometimes do something similar with my own growth. I've done a lot of reading about spiritual growth and emotional healing. I'm familiar with what it means to be healthy. But much of the time, instead of investing in self-examination and real change, I put out some green gravel and act as though I've changed. Instead of working through my anger, I act mature. Instead of revealing my inner self to others, I act honest. Instead of tackling

my selfishness and self-absorption, I act unselfish. Instead of "listening to my life" (to borrow Frederick Buechner's phrase) and learning from it, I pick up nuggets of wisdom from books and pass them on to others.

Like the man with the green gravel, I skip the effort and try to pretend the results are real. Although, through my vain attempts, God is always there calling me back to this true purpose for my life. It is through the Holy Spirit's gentle prodding that I realize unless I give up on the masquerade of growth, I'm not going to do much real growing at all. It's hard for grass to grow underneath all those rocks!

Prayer: Lord, help me to act on the lessons you have taught me. It is only through your strength that I can achieve honest growth.

*Nothing is more beautiful
than the loveliness of the
woods before sunrise*
—George Washington Carver

I was raised to appreciate fine music, but one of my favorite singers couldn't carry a tune in a bucket. He was a high-school friend, a gifted young man who excelled in art and English, earned straight As, and presided over many organizations. Music was not his strong suit; he had trouble singing two consecutive notes in the same key. But he loved to sing! And I loved singing with him, because his enjoyment was so infectious. He taught me the truth of Chesterton's statement that, "anything worth doing is worth doing badly."

That does not mean there should be no standards or that we should do less than our best in any given area. Shoddy or lazy work is an insult to our Creator and a betrayal of the gifts He put in us. The act of doing something well can also bring great satisfaction and pleasure.

But I sometimes wonder if our contemporary emphasis on excellence is robbing us of the joy of doing things just for fun— not to mention preventing the growth that comes with trying

something new. Many of us, if we aren't talented or skilled in a particular pursuit, tend to hang back from learning or even trying it.

It takes courage to do something badly and enjoy it—to dare to sing off key, to produce clumsy paintings, or to stretch our uncoordinated muscles to play softball. But the benefits, I've discovered, are wonderful. It's hard to take myself too seriously when I know I'm not a genius and that knowledge also makes me more tolerant of others' less-than-perfect efforts. But the chief benefit, I believe, is the God-given joy of using my eyes, using my muscles, using my voice—not because I'm good at it, but because it's worth doing!

Prayer: God, thank you that you have given me talents to use for your glory. Thank you, also, for the joy found in exploring new skills.

Spring is sprung;

the grass is riz—

I wonder where

them flowers is?

—Old rhyme

We planted beans in a little cup, watered them, and put them in a warm window to wait. Five minutes later she was leaning on the windowsill, disappointed that nothing was happening. And although I smiled at her vague concept of time, I knew how she felt.

I have spent a lot of my life in the time warp between planting and sprouting, between making my move and seeing results, between doing what I could and knowing whether I did the right thing. I apply for the job, but I won't hear yea or nay for days or even weeks. I invite a new acquaintance to lunch, not knowing whether friendship will flower. I have the biopsy, but they'll call me in a few days with the results. I work on a committee, teach a class, or pray for someone, but only time will tell whether my efforts have made a difference.

Whether it's filled with excited anticipation or fearful dread, waiting is hard. And it's especially hard when I realize that I may not see results even in my lifetime.

Something deep inside me clamors for closure. Like my three-year-old, I don't want to wait on God's perfect timing and see how the

future unfolds; I want to know now! But God usually doesn't work that way. Much of the time, I'm stuck with waiting. But while I wait, maybe there are some things I need to ask myself:

- Have I really done all I can do—including pray?
- Is there something God wants me to learn while I'm waiting—about patience, trust, or overcontrol?
- Are there matters I need to attend to in the meantime? Is my frustration distracting me from other matters that need my attention?
- Do I need a perspective adjustment? Have I fallen into the child's trap of thinking the only reality is what happens *now*?

Prayer: Lord, Psalm 90 reminds me that "a thousand years in Your sight are like yesterday when it is past." Give me the gift of Your perspective whenever I feel caught in a time warp.

Imagination [is] . . .
Reason in her most
exalted mood.

——William Wordsworth

My six-year-old daughter is a spinner of tales. She loves to dream up fantasies and tell them to me. She also embellishes her factual reports. A simple report about what happened at school will gradually evolve into a delightful piece of fiction replete with unicorns.

And that poses a dilemma for me. I believe in nurturing our God-given creativity and imagination. I'm convinced we learn to solve problems in our lives by coming up with ideas that depart from what we've always done and thought. And I love my daughter's stories. Her imagination brings me delight. But I also believe in honesty, in speaking the truth to myself and others. Without honesty, our creativity is of little help in solving problems, because problems have to be faced before they can be solved.

This isn't a problem for children only. Do you ever struggle to find a balance between what is and what might be? Do you ever wonder at what point a positive attitude becomes denial or when rigorous honesty becomes hard-edged fatalism? For me, it's easy to tip the balance—to live in a dream world or to get trapped in the cynical realism of thinking things will never change.

I think the key to balance here is to realize that imagination and realism aren't the polar opposites we make them out to be. Surely honesty must recognize the power of dreams, and the best imaginative tales hold a clear mirror to truth. Imagination is best used in a way that opens up God's truths and reality, not runs from it.

To help us both find that balance, my daughter and I have set up a practice of calling a "reality check" after the story. She's free to embellish her tales at will, but I'm also free to call for a more down-to-earth account when I need it. It's too early to know if this practice will help us keep in touch with what is without losing heart for what might be, but it shows promise.

Prayer: Dear Lord, teach me to nurture the gift of imagination without losing touch with Your truth.

*If you are walking on
the Decatur Road
when winter turns spring,
you will probably slip
and fall and hurt yourself.
It is a mud-happy
stretch at this turn,
and if you are not careful
you could very well slide
all the way into Decatur.*

—Joe Coomer

The old-time preachers called it backsliding. And that's exactly how it feels when you've made significant progress, really grown in some area, only to fall back into your old habits.

You've stuck to your eating and exercise plan, and your faithfulness has been rewarded by toned muscles and a smaller dress size. Then one day you're a slug in front of the TV, mainlining ice cream again.

You've disciplined yourself to handle each piece of paper only once, filing papers away or tossing them as they hit your desk. And you've reveled in the sense of order—until one day you put aside a paper to "think about it," and before you know it you're shuffling through a haystack of correspondence just to find an eraser.

It's an irritating and discouraging experience, but it doesn't have to send you all the way back to the mud puddle any more than a cold snap after Easter has to signal a new ice age. You always have the choice to stop your slide by reaching for help and changing your direction. And the old-time preachers had a word for that too—*repentance.*

Don't let any "holy roller" connotations get you down here. *Repent* isn't a browbeating term; it's a promise of hope. It means that with God's help, no matter how far back you've sloshed, you can climb out of the puddle and move forward again.

It's not easy. You have to face what has happened, face your own weakness, confess it to God and to others, and ask for help. It may take awhile to climb back up to where you were. But what a relief to have the chance to do it!

Prayer: Lord, give me the insight to look behind the old clichés to discover truth — and hope that your grace and mercy can help me become the person you would have me to be.

The excessiveness of life
is the best sacrament we
could ask for, a hint of how
powerful, how determined,
and how excessive You are.

— *Andrew Greeley*

My part of the world is really going all out on spring this year. Explosions of dogwoods and redbud. Fields blanketed in wildflowers. Lawns breaking out in an impossible, eye-popping green. Even the bird's song is exuberant and unrestrained—*Tweet!*

In a way, I expect spring to be energetic and excessive. It seems normal. So if I don't take time to listen, I might lose the message: there's nothing inherently wrong with excess, and there's a time in life for going all out.

I need to hear that message especially right now, at my particular (middle-aged) time of life. Like many people, I was an extremist when I was young—pouring myself into my loves and my enthusiasms with seemingly endless energy. But as I matured, I had to back off. I realized there are limits to my time and my energy; I learned to assess my resources realistically and reserve my "big guns" for the most important battles.

The trouble is sometimes I've gotten that message wrong. Instead of choosing my battles, I've ended up putting my guns in cold

storage. At times I'm in danger of becoming too careful with myself and my energies—not reaching out, not taking risks, not investing myself fully in anything. It's easy to mistake meanness for moderation, stinginess for self-discipline, laziness for maturity, fear for wisdom.

And that's why I've got to get into my head the message of a burgeoning spring. God is a God of abundance, even a God of excess. He doesn't do things halfway. And while He wants me to grow up and learn wisdom, I don't think He means for me to back off from risk. There really are times to go all out.

Prayer: God, only in Your love can I learn the balance of choosing wisely but investing myself fully. Teach me the gift of excessiveness when it comes to faith, hope, love, and joy.

Rain, rain, go away . . .

—*Nursery rhyme*

It's one of those weeks when everybody seems depressed.
Rain has been drizzling and pouring for five days straight (too many
April showers). Bad news is all over the TV: a slumping economy, a
virus going around, too much work for everybody. The convenience
store clerk is frowning and distracted. The doctor's receptionist is
irritable. My daughter is impossible. And I long to talk to someone
who's openly, sincerely upbeat.

Some days it really does seem as if someone has thrown a
wet blanket over the whole world. Whether it's one person's attitude
or some sort of general malaise, times like that are murder to
get through.

So how do we get through them? To a certain extent, of course,
we need to just grit our teeth and hang on. Chances are the rain will
eventually stop, people will get well, the economy will swing the
other way, our hormone level will change.

But things don't always get better. Floods, depressions, wars,
and epidemics really happen. Relationships sour. People turn on each

other. Institutions fall apart. So I'm wary of depending too much on "the sun will come out tomorrow." Probably it will. But what if it doesn't?

I think Jesus had a much more realistic and workable approach: "In the world you will have tribulation," He warned, "but be of good cheer, I have overcome the world" (John 16:33) If we depend entirely on the world around us to bring us happiness and fulfillment, we'll be at the mercy of gray days and sour circumstances and the cataclysms of history.

Prayer: God, You said there would be days like this! You also made it clear I don't have to be at their mercy. Teach me to know You, to lean on You, to focus on Your light within me. (Meanwhile, if it fits Your plan, how about some sunshine?)

I firmly believe that nature

brings solace in all troubles

——Anne Frank

They've been married forty years this spring. Overall, it's been a fruitful union—two kids, three grandkids, a sizable contingent of friends and colleagues, and a slate of satisfying accomplishments. Despite nagging worries about health and kids and retirement, they're more or less content—and proud of themselves for coming this far.

But the fight they had this week was the same fight they've had off and on since the week after their wedding.

She likes to talk.

He doesn't.

She gets her feelings hurt.

He feels pressured.

Both get irritated. Sparks fly.

Yes, they've changed over the years. Circumstances have changed them. In some ways, they've worked at changing. Certainly they've adapted to each other and learned to work through problems. But even now there are issues they have never resolved. For the most part, they've learned to just accept—but not always.

In a sense, it's a little depressing. Surely after all those years, they would have put those problems to bed. But in another sense, they give me hope that it's possible to persist and forgive and keep hoping even when some issues resist resolution. They remind me that it's possible to live a satisfying, full live even with unsolved problems and unresolved conflicts.

How else can we flawed human beings hope to live together?

Prayer: Lord, I need both discernment and commitment for my relationships to work. Help me to know where to push for resolution and where to accept our differences.

Thomas Kinkade

Fair daffodils,

we weep to see You

haste away so soon.

—*Robert Herrick*

Just a few weeks ago, the whole town seemed touched with magic. Trees bubbled with bloom. Parking lot dividers and corporate landscaping waved with tulips and irises. Vacant lots sported wildflower weeds. Even the slums were spruced up with flowers.

And now, so soon, the magic has faded. Floral confetti litters the ground around trees as branches shed their blossoms and get down to the business of being green. Parking lots are parking lots again. Vacant lots have been mowed. The slums have settled back into their everyday despair.

And it's a little sad, this fading of spring—almost like a little death in the middle of life. In such a short time the magic is set aside; life turns ordinary again.

Maybe it's an obvious metaphor, but the magic in our lives and our relationships fades too.

I remember times when romance bloomed along with the daffodils, when my newborn and I discovered together the wonder of a caterpillar and an acorn, when a new friendship unfolded in the

sunshine of acceptance and shared confidence. And all that fresh love changed, faded—either into the energetic, exhausting business of growing or the withering heat of conflict and boredom.

Some relationships faded. But some (thank God!) bore wonderful fruit. It was during that season of magic that the foundation of a healthy and thriving bond was formed.

Prayer: Lord, the magic always fades. That seems to be the way You've made things. Teach me to savor the freshness of new love and new relationships but to let go of the magic with good grace and to put my energy into growing.

Thomas
Kinkade

Creativity is inventing,
experimenting, growing,
taking risks, breaking
rules, making mistakes,
and having fun.

—Mary Lou Cook

It's the one complaint guaranteed to raise my hackles:
"But I can't . . ."

"I can't draw."

"I can't sing."

"I can't do math."

Whether it comes from adult or child, I bristle when I
hear it. And I hate to have to say it! I was raised to be a "can do"
kind of person. Deep down, I'm convinced I can do anything if I
put my mind to it. Having to say "I can't" smells like failure to me.
It feels humiliating.

And it is true that "I can't" easily becomes a self-fulfilling,
self-limiting prophecy. (As my grandfather used to say, why would
you want to prove yourself wrong?) I've seen people robbed of joy
in whole categories of life because they told themselves "I can't."
Sometimes "I can't" really means "I'm afraid to try," and it gets in
the way of growth.

But I'm gradually learning (the hard way) that "can do" can be as damaging as "I can't." Maybe I really can do anything if I'm willing to make the tradeoffs. But the tradeoffs are significant, and in many cases the payoffs are just not worth it. I am a human being—subject to the limitations of talent and time and choices made. That means that in many situations, learning to say an honest "I can't" is not a form of self-sabotage but a necessary lesson in humility. Very often when I accept that *I* can't, I find that God can use my limitations to reveal his power through those circumstances.

To rephrase the famous Serenity Prayer:

Prayer: Lord, grant me the serenity to accept the things I can't . . . The courage to do the things I can . . . And the wisdom to know the difference.

*And lo, I am with
you always, even to
the end of the age.*

Matthew 28:20

Want to see a teacher explode?

Just try making a remark about working "only" six hours a day—or "only" nine months a year. If you are not injured, you'll be quickly enlightened about what happens behind the scenes of the teaching profession—curriculum development, lesson preparation, conferences, grading, career development, and much more.

Of course, that is true of almost any pursuit; a large portion of the work goes on behind the scenes. Behind every corporate report lurk weeks of research, writing, and emptying the coffeepot in the middle of the night. Behind every speech hide hours of scribbling, editing, and even declaiming before the mirror. Behind every clean house kneels a householder with a vacuum cleaner and a bottle of all-purpose cleaner.

It's a mistake to assume that the only work that counts is work that is immediately visible. But I think I do that a lot with God. Either consciously or unconsciously, I evaluate God's work in my

life according to whether I can see progress or feel His presence.
If I can't, I often assume He's not on the job.

But there's so much about God's work I can't see—at least not
until later. What feels like intense conflict may be His preparation for
a new era in my life. What feels like spiritual dryness may be His
strategy for drawing me closer to Him Ordinary events may actually
be a series of sacred opportunities that I'm too dull to perceive.
In other words, I often can't see what God is doing in my life
but that doesn't mean nothing's happening!

And I know all that—so why can't I remember it?

Prayer: Father, grant me the perception to see Your
work in my life—and the faith to know You're working even
when I can't see it.

For there is hope for a tree,
If it is cut down, that it will
sprout again, And that its
tender shoots will not cease.

—Job 14:7

Can't be fixed: a child's face stares bleakly up at me over the plastic shards of a shattered toy.

Can't be fixed: the giant oak lies among the hurricanes debris, its roots upended helplessly.

Can't be fixed: the man and the woman stare across the distance between them, shocked into silence by brutal words finally uttered.

Some things in life can be patched up, shored up, repaired, or redone. But some wounds are too grievous, some blows too shattering, some rifts too wide to be pulled back together. Some experiences — a divorce, a betrayal, abuse, neglect—leave us permanently wounded, our psyches disfigured. We live, we go on, but we're not really fixed.

Yet I believe there is an alternate plan for things that can't be fixed. It won't work for shattered plastic, but this plan can make an astonishing difference in living, growing things like trees and people. I've seen it in a new shoot growing from a shattered stump, in the faces of a couple whose counseling sessions are finally showing some

progress. I've seen it in people who have hit bottom and admitted their own helplessness, only to begin growing again from there.

As far as I can see, God's strategy for broken trees and limbs and lives and souls is not repair but growth, not being patched up but being granted the gift of starting over. Through God's grace and mercy our broken places are ultimately used to provide a fresh start to make us whole again.

Can't be fixed—but can be reborn.

Can't be fixed—but can be made new.

Prayer: Lord, the older I get, the more I feel like a patched-up collection of old wounds and badly healed scars. I give You my broken pieces Father. And I beg You not to fix me, but to make me new again.

Thomas
Kinkade

God is great,
and therefore He will be
sought; He is good, and
therefore He will be found.

—Anonymous

As a person who sunburns under a full moon, I have never qualified as a sun worshiper. So now—in this era of sunscreen—I get a certain amount of satisfaction watching the in crowd hide from the rays. Even now, in spring, the articles start to appear, urging us to get prepared for "sun season."

According to the article I just read, protecting ourselves in these days of ozone depletion is a full-time occupation. We're supposed to put on high-octane sunscreen first thing in the morning and replenish it during the day because it is almost impossible to hide from the sun. Ordinary T-shirts won't keep out those UV rays. Hats and umbrellas don't keep out reflected sun. Only a good sunscreen, applied conscientiously, offers adequate protection from wrinkles and skin cancer and "horrid' age spots. Even with sunscreen, we're advised to stay indoors between the hours of eleven and three.

All of this sounds a little scary—and it's a lot of trouble. But if I turn the whole picture around a little, I get a vivid picture of how God's love works. We talk about seeking God, when in reality his love, like those UV rays, is always seeking us. He is positive, powerful energy that seeks me out and helps me grow (no horrid age spots here). His love surrounds me all the time, even when I can't see it. If it can't reach me directly, it will find me another way. There's only one way I can avoid its effects—by choosing to say no to it—and even that doesn't always work.

Prayer: Lord, You surround me and seek me out even when I think I'm seeking You. I want to bask in Your love and mercy.

Let the little children come to Me, and do not forbid them; for of such is the kingdom of heaven

—Matthew 19:14

When was the last time you took off your shoes and played in the sprinkler? Or took advantage of a summer rainshower and walked around the block, letting yourself get soaked to the skin? "I can't do that anymore; I'm a responsible adult." Yes, and you're probably missing out on the pure delight of being a kid. Watch the children next time you're in a park. Do they worry about what people will think? Of course not. That's something that we learn as we get older and gradually "put away childish things," as the apostle Paul said in the New Testament letter to the Corinthians.

Is that what Paul meant? I doubt it! Put away immaturity, maybe. Leave behind elementary ideas of faith as you grow in your journey, probably. But if Jesus Christ himself told His followers to "come unto me as little children," and "whoever does not receive the Kingdom of God as a little child will not enter it," then there must be something to the idea of maintaining childlike wonder and spontaneity. Children respond naturally to beauty and joy, and they

don't hold back when they are excited about something. They possess an inner freedom
that permits them to be outwardly enthusiastic about life and the joy of God's creation without fear of criticism.

Wouldn't it be great to get some of that back? What if you threw caution to the wind and took a walk in the rain or climbed a tree for no good reason or went to the park and hopped on a swing? Sure, you might get a strange look from somebody, but who cares? You're a grown-up, and you can do anything you want to.

Prayer: Lord, help me today to see life through the eyes of a child. Instead of attempting to look perfect, help me to give myself the grace to be spontaneous and free in my enjoyment of Your world.

Thomas
Kinkade

Today a new sun
rises for me; everything
lives, everything is
animated, everything
seems to speak
to me of my passion,
everything invites me
to cherish it.

—Anne De Lenclos

Nothing has had quite the same impact on me as standing on a winter beach, watching a fog bank roll in over the Gulf of Mexico. A wall of gray, it moved in so fast I actually watched it eating up the blue sky and the emerald water, rendering the horizon a whitewash of colorless gray. Closer and closer it moved, until finally, the gray enveloped the ground on which I stood. The waves at my feet only moments before were sparkling with the sun's reflection, now were a turbulent foam of brine.

Although I've spent years of my life watching the ebb and flow of Gulf tides, I've witnessed the fog bank phenomenon only once. One moment I was standing in the warmth of the South Texas sun; the next I was surrounded by a surreal world of minimal visibility. As I watched the wall of gray roll in I didn't move, knowing this was as rare as catching sight of a shooting star. Although eerie, the experience wasn't frightening. Rather, it was captivating—as if living inside a moment of magic—much like the transforming grace

of God. At times God's grace is a presence so real that the moment is tangible. Then again, it is as ethereal as a fog bank recomposing an expanse of sea. But always present, always interrupting our ordinary lives with moments of wonder—if we only take the time to see.

Prayer: Lord, open my eyes today to the moments of wonder you lay before me. Whether an unexpected tear or a much-needed laugh, open my eyes to the gift of life I have in this moment.

Earth's crammed
with heaven
And every common
bush afire with God;
But only he who sees
takes off his shoes,
The rest sit round it
and pluck blackberries.
—*Elizabeth Barrett Browning*

If you've never read the book, then maybe you've seen Cecil B. DeMille's epic movie *The Ten Commandments.* Do you remember the scene when Moses went to the top of the mountain to meet with God? Moses met the Almighty in the form of a burning bush, and he was informed by the voice of God that where he was standing was holy ground. His response was that of reverence, awe, and holy fear; he took off his shoes.

The Japanese know about reverence and respect; they take off their shoes when they enter a house. It's not something we Americans do out of any particular courtesy, if we do it at all, it's to be comfortable or because our feet hurt. I love what Browning says in her poem. All around us is God's creation, earth crammed with heaven. Do we really respect it, revere it, and hold it in awe? Or do we simply take it for granted?

We live in a time of great awareness of Earth's frailty. Some are afraid that if we don't do something radical, we won't be able to pass on the beauty of God's creation to our descendants. Most of us are

doing more than ever to make adjustments to help the earth—recycling, buying eco-friendly products, and generally "thinking green."

To revere the earth and its beauty as the wondrous work of God, to honor its loveliness with awe—that's something I can take my shoes off for.

Prayer: O, Lord, I will respect the earth out of gratitude for its beauty and wonder. Thank You for the gift of Your creation.

*Then God saw everything
that He had made, and
indeed it was very good.*

—Genesis 1:31

Cold days. Long nights. December. A season of waiting. Waiting for the first cup of coffee to brew on a cold, dreary morning. Waiting for clouds to clear. Waiting for the first snowfall after the ground has turned brown. Waiting for the holidays with the newspaper daily reminding me how many shopping days are left until Christmas.

I've never been very patient with waiting. In fact, I hate to wait. I fume when placed on hold by a reservations clerk. I feel the tension creeping in my shoulders when waiting for slow-moving traffic on slick wet roads. Whether waiting for a doctors appointment or waiting in a grocery checkout line, I like things to happen *now*.

So the phrase "wait on the Lord" has always been a bit baffling to me. Why? What exactly was the psalmist waiting for?

The psalmist knew something I'm only now beginning to appreciate—waiting implies promise. We don't wait for something unless there's something we're waiting for. We don't wait for Christmas, unless Chrsitmas means something to us. We don't wait in

traffic, unless there's somewhere we want to go. If we didn't drink coffee, we wouldn't wait for the coffee to brew.

Waiting on the Lord is acknowledging God's timing, not ours. Waiting on the Lord is giving up our need to control, to make things happen. Waiting on the Lord is anticipating God's acting in our lives. Waiting on the Lord is faith.

Prayer: Lord, help me to wait on your timing.

Do not withhold good
from those to whom it is due,
When it is in the power of
your hand to do so.

—*Proverbs 3:27*

"I just want you to know that your child was delightful in the nursery this morning." "You have a wonderful way with people, and I admire that." "Your house is so warm and welcoming." "You told that guy the truth on that deal, and I respect you for it."

Wouldn't it be great to hear things like that all the time? How many times do you think about saying something encouraging or uplifting to someone else, but you just don't feel comfortable? It's a risk; what if they think you're just trying to butter them up? You could come off sounding insincere. So you keep it to yourself, instead, and the encouraging word never gets said. Oh, maybe you think about it later and have every good intention of writing a note, but you never get it written. Time goes by and you've lost that moment forever.

It's not just words, of course. There are times when you might see a situation that could use something—time, money, skills— that you possess and could share. It might be as simple as offering to drive an elderly neighbor to the store or washing a friend's car when

they're too busy to take care of it. Or it might be a case where you have extra money and know of someone who's struggling financially. What a joy to send an anonymous gift!

Think of the times that someone has given you something right when you needed it—an encouraging note or phone call, a helping hand with a project, or a few bucks when you were strapped for cash. It meant a lot to you, didn't it? Don't miss the opportunity to give to someone else.

Prayer: Show me, Lord, how I can give of myself to someone else today.

Listen to this, O Job;
Stand still and consider the
wondrous works of God.

—Job 37:14

I'll tell you where I'd like to be right now . . . either standing on a peak in the Rocky Mountains or at the shoreline of the Pacific Ocean. Doesn't that sound wonderful? Getting away to a place where nature is right out in front of us can really help to clear our minds of all the stuff that clutters and keeps us from being focused. And it seems to be so much easier to focus on God when we are someplace like the mountains or the beach. The Rockies and the Pacific Ocean would sure qualify as "wondrous works of God," don't you think? In the book of Job, God's characteristics are renumerated as Job's friends attempt to counsel him through his trials. Notice that the friend in the story tells Job to "stand still and consider the wondrous works of God."

It's easy to stand still when you're gazing at the Pacific Ocean or breathing mountain air. It's tough to do it when you're in the middle of a crazy work day or surrounded by the demands of a family. But aren't those things also the wondrous works of God?

The innocent face of a child, the familiar voice of a spouse, the steadiness and reliability of a coworker—all these things remind us that we are not alone, that our Heavenly Father is at work in the midst of us. That's a good thing to hold on to when the going gets rough.

Prayer: Today I will "stand still," if only in my mind, to consider the wondrous things of God around me.

Thomas Kinkade

*It hain't no use to
grumble and complain,
It's jest as easy to rejoice;
When God sorts out the
weather and sends rain,
Why rain's my choice.*

—J. W. Riley

The morning is rainy where I live, and though I prefer sunshine to rain most days, I'm aware of rain's purpose in creation. Where I live, spring and summer rains are frequent, and the landscape shows its lovely greening effects in the light hues of spring to the darker shades of August. Trees are leafy, good for providing shade on a hot, bright day. If you've seen pictures of Ireland, you know how green it is over there. I found out why when I visited a few years back. It rains almost every day, even in the summer. But it's rarely torrential or violent. Often the rain comes down in gentle showers or mist, what the Irish call "soft" days.

Rain does soften the day and quiet the world. Sun is loud— it just calls for shouting. Notice the birds; even they are quiet when the rain falls.

Now, I'm one who enjoys a boisterous summer day, with children laughing and birds chirping and even cars honking. But it's nice to have a rainy day every once in a while. It's a good time to get quiet, to be reflective, and to slow down just a bit.

What happens to you on a rainy day? Do you see it as an intrusion, as a foiler of plans or an inconvenience? Or do you accept a rainy day as God's way of getting you to slow down? Rain waters the grass and makes the flowers grow. Can it give some refreshment to your spirit?

Prayer: Instead of complaining about the rain, I will be thankful and appreciate the way it quiets my world.

*He deserves paradise
who makes his
companions laugh.*

—Anonymous

There's nothing better than a good laugh. Don't you love being around people who see humor in everyday life? We need to laugh. The book of Proverbs tells us that laughter does good like a medicine. Even medical science tells us now that laughing is good for us; it releases endorphins, chemicals that get the blood flowing and increase our general sense of well-being. In totally unscientific terms, it feels darn good! Author Norman Cousins wrote about the healing power of laughter in his book *Anatomy of an Illness*, in which he related his battle with disease and his self-administered treatments of Marx Brothers movies and "I Love Lucy" reruns.

You and I may not need a cure for a physical illness, but what about a cure for the summer blahs? Stuck in an office or at home with the kids, sometimes it's hard to see the humor in daily life. Children, of course, can be a great source of laughter. When your kids say something funny, do you let go with a belly laugh or do you hold back? In your work, are you around people who automatically see the funny side of a situation? What about you? Would you be

described as someone who has a good sense of humor?

I love what Reinhold Niebuhr said about laughter. He was an acclaimed theologian, one of the twentieth century's greatest thinkers and the originator of what has become known as the "Serenity Prayer." His advice to those who sat under him? "All you earnest young men out to save the world . . . please, have a laugh."

Isn't that great? We can get so serious about life sometimes that we can wear ourselves—and each other—out. What's your H.Q. (Humor Quotient)? If you're reading this, chances are you're taking a serious look at your own life. That's great. Just let yourself laugh your head off from time to time. Nobody has ever died from an endorphin overdose.

Prayer: Father, thank You for this gift of laughter.

I grow old . . .

I grow old . . .

I shall wear the bottoms

of my trousers rolled.

Shall I part my

hair behind?

Do I dare to eat a peach?

I shall wear white flannel

trousers, and walk

upon the beach.

I have heard the mermaids

singing, each to each.

—*T. S. Eliot, "The Love Song of*

J. Alfred Prufrock"

There was a time when faith came easily. When the touch of God in my life was new and his presence was as intimate as my own rhythmic breathing. I remeber times when prayer was a spontaneous response to the fullness within, when my heart was full of promise and my faith was one of ready answers. Then something changed. I was confused, bewildered. I was doing all the same things, seeking in all the same ways, yet something within me has died. God had become distant, remote, and unreachable. I would read the saying on posters or cards, "When God seems distant, who moved?" and feel guilty–or angry–as if an invisible cosmic finger pointed at me accusingly.

Then I came across a line in a book by John Vannorsdall with which my heart resonated: "We heard so much about the presence of God that we were unprepared for the long absence of God." The absence of God. There. The words were spoken. I was not the only one who had experienced the absence of God. The absence of God was through no lack of spiritual performance on my part, simply an ebb and flow of the spiritual life.

Theologians and thinkers through the centuries have written of the dark night of the soul, the spiritual wall, the wintry seasons of the heart. I have no come to understand that wintry spirituality is as true to the biblical tradition as the intimacy of the incarnation. I am no less faithful for acknowledging the questions without answers, the doubts that hover like low hanging clouds, and tears that obscure my view of a hidden God. For it is only in the winter of the heart, the season when all is seemingly dormant, that depth can take root, compassion is born, and honesty seeker, how can he be worthy of my devotion?

I am no stranger to the winter of the heart. but I am in good company. Others have gone before me through the seasons of faith.

Prayer: Hear my prayer, O Lord, and give ear to my cry; do not be silent at my tears; for I am a stranger with You.

— *Psalm 39:12*

He ate and drank
the precious words,
His spirit grew robust;
He knew no more
that he was poor,
Nor that his frame was dust.
He danced along the
dingy days,
And this bequest of wings
Was but a book.
What liberty a loosened
spirit brings.

—Emily Dickinson

Here I sit. A rainy weekday morning. The dreariness is contagious. I know the rain is good for farmers and plants. But I'm not a farmer and unlike plants, the rain dampens my spirit, not my roots.

How do we muster any enthusiasm on days like today? Days of downcast spirits, a heavy heart, and responsibilities that feel overwhelming? Even the writers of the Old Testament occasionlly needed reminders, so after years of oral tradition they finally wrote the words down that we now find in the Bible.

Today I need to hear this Old Testament reminder: "The Lord will open to you His good treasure." As I read these words, I wonder what treasure can be found in rainy days, dreary skies, and melancholy moods? The answer softly comes to me–reassurance Reassurance that I'm not in this alone. Just as the fathers of my faith, I'm starting in the right place. I'm coming to a moment of quiet and seeking the presence of God. Only he can bring order to my confusion, encouragement to my work-weary world, and

enthusiasm to my dreary heart. So God, this one's for you. This day and all that lays before me I put in your hands. The rain. The fatigue. The responsibilities. The part of me that feels stretched beyond my limits. This day I give to you, knowing your limits are infinite and your love is inexhaustable.

Prayer: Lord, reframe my thinking as I go into this day, and let me learn from my tendency to overcommit myself. I give you this dreary day and my heavy heart–and ask that with the rain come showers of your grace . . . in my thinking, my working, my living.

As a white candle
in a holy place,
So is the beauty
of an aged face.

Joseph Campbell

We live in a culture that reveres its youth and ignores its elders. Nearly every other culture does the opposite and is the richer for it. We are the poorer for having put our grandparents in retirement villages, far away from grandchildren who don't know the wisdom they are missing by not having Grandpa and Grandma around.

The things we can learn from our elders are limitless. They were born in a time that was very different from our own, and their perspective on life can be of great value as we struggle with our daily lives in this fast-paced, unsettling era. Imagine for a moment: a person born at the end of the last century would have lived through the First World War, the Great Depression, yet another World War, and the suburbanization of America. A telephone would have been a rare thing in the home of their childhood; now their grandchildren can have phones in their cars, their purses, and their pockets.

Life has changed at a speed never seen before in human history. More than ever, we need the sagacity of those who lived in a slower time.

Are the elders all gone from your life? Look around— people who have lived rich, full lives are sitting near you in a pew, at the train station, and in a nursing home. Ask them questions. Listen, really listen, to their answers. Let them teach you with their stories. Learn from their Godly wisdom, and rejoice in the things our Heavenly Father can teach you through his precious saints.

Prayer: Lord, help me to listen to the wisdom of the elders around me, and remember the ones who have gone home to be with You.

How far that little
candle throws his beams!
So shines a good deed in
a naughty world.
—Shakespeare,
The Merchant of Venice

Somewhere between the lingering shadows of autumn days and the tulips and daffodils of early spring lies a siege of short days, long nights, and nasty weather. And despite knowing that this season, too, shall pass, I still succumb to the haunting spell of winter with those nagging feelings that it will always and forever be this way. Spring will never come. The skies will never clear. I will never be thin. And whatever difficult circumstances I'm facing now will never be resolved. Dark thoughts with circular repetition crowd out clear thinking just as dark skies dim the sun. Those nagging thoughts are my winter myth.

Sometimes I'm caught between what my heart is feeling and what my head is thinking. And the result is fatigue, restlessness, or depression. Knowing winter will not last forever does not make me feel any better, give me more energy, or even brighten my day, just as knowing my circumstances are not always and forever does not lessen my anxiety.

Connecting what I *know* to be true with the knot in my stomach and the concerns of my heart is seldom within my power. But it *is* within God's power. Giving God my tomorrows, seeking his presence in this day disarms the winter darkness and frees me from the lure of the winter myth. Only God is always and forever—and he is trustworthy for my todays.

Prayer: God, take my dark thoughts and bring Your warming sun into my winter spirit. You know the concerns, the fears, the myths that cloud my world. Let me hear Your gentle truth today that I may walk into my winter world wrapped in the cloak of Your loving spirit.

Thomas
Kinkade

*It's easier to focus
on the one brown
patch rather than the
expanse of green lawn
surrounding it.*

I talked with a friend the other day. She told me that she and her husband just paid off their mortgage. I was amazed. Now that was an accomplishment!

"How did you celebrate?" I asked her.

"What do you mean?" she responded.

"Didn't you make a big deal out of it?"

"Not really. It was just another day."

We, as a society, don't celebrate enough. We certainly do enough complaining, though. You only have to watch the evening news or read the daily paper to see where our emphasis lies: on the pain, the negative, and the suffering.

It's important for us to look for small blessings small accomplishments to celebrate. And if we can't find any of those, we can make some up. Some parenting books even recommend each person have one day (a week or month) designated as his or her special day. That person gets to choose what's for dinner and receives special treatment the entire day. You could even make a banner or

have the person wear a crown. "Queen" or "King for a Day." Sounds hokey, but the person wearing the crown feels pretty good, especially if it's a young child.

God has given us so much. The small, daily blessings are his gifts to us—reminders of His love. It's a good idea to make a big deal of any small thing: getting a call from a friend, a good school paper, a clean house, or paying off a credit card.

Prayer: Lord, thank You for Your blessings. Help me to see the small reminders of You that surround me daily.

Finally, brethren, whatever things are true, whatever things are noble, whatever things are just, whatever things are pure, whatever things are lovely, whatever things are of good report, if there be any virtue and if there is anything praiseworthy—meditate on these things.

—Philippians 4:8

Have you ever noticed how good you feel when you're around people who seem enthused with life? I do. I don't think it's coincidence either. I believe God planned the world in such a way that we would feel good when around the beautiful, the pure, and the just. In fact, I think we can look at our souls as if God programmed two very opposing feelings within every human being.

The first is called a "cup of joy." Whenever we drink from this cup we feel great, incredible, and happy. Things that surround us, such as our loved ones, the beauty of nature, and the miracle of creation, make us drink from this cup.

But God also gave us a "cup of sorrow." And He did so because this was the only way we could tell what the cup of joy tasted like. He arranged for the cup of joy to taste imminently better than the cup of sorrow, but we would never know that until we tasted the cup of sorrow.

Unfortunately, we have one problem: The human race has become hooked on the cup of sorrow. In fact, we're so preoccupied with how bad it tastes that it seems we have completely forgotten about the cup of joy.

Meditating on the good in the world, on the beauty of God's creation and joyful sounds of singing will help us to rediscover our own cups of joy. If we redirect our focus to these things and contemplate them, we will be drinking from the cup of joy and be reminded how wonderful it is to be alive

Prayer: God, help me to find the joy in all that surrounds me today. Help me to be mindful of your creation and the beauty of being content.

NANETTE

Thomas Kinkade

The heavens declare

the glory of God;

And the firmament

shows His handiwork.

—Psalm 19:1

The heavens are a marvel to me. Surely, they are the finest example of God's handiwork. I spent one fall on the north shore of Lake Superior, far away from any cities. Here the night skies were breathtakingly beautiful. The stars seemed so bright, so close I could almost touch them. An added bonus was the frequent displays of northern lights. "The best in years," I was told by locals.

I was driving from Canada to Minnesota with a friend late one night when I saw my first aurora borealis. That experience remains etched in my mind. The northern lights are incredible to behold. No matter how descriptive one can be, no one knows what it's like until he or she has seen them firsthand.

My first thought upon viewing the display—pinks, purples, reds, greens—in the night sky was, *These aren't subtle at all. You can't miss the curtains of colors that fall from the heavens.* My second thought was, *It's a miracle!* And my third thought, *God can paint!*

Prayer: Lord, when I look upon the night sky, help me to see Your creativity in its display.

Thomas Kinkade